WATERBIRDS *of Australia*

First published in 2010 by New Holland Publishers (Australia) Pty Ltd
Sydney • Auckland • London • Cape Town

www.newholland.com.au

1/66 Gibbes Street Chatswood NSW 2067 Australia
218 Lake Road Northcote Auckland New Zealand
86 Edgware Road London W2 2EA United Kingdom
80 McKenzie Street Cape Town 8001 South Africa

A record of this book is available at the National Library of Australia

ISBN 9781877069826

Publisher: Diane Jardine
Editor: Mary Trewby
Cover and internal design: Emma Gough
Publishing manager: Lliane Clarke
Production manager: Olga Dementiev
Printer: Toppan Leefung Printing Ltd

Front cover: Greater Sand Plover
Back Cover: Black-winged Stilt
Front Flap: Australian Pelican and Pied Heron
Endpapers: Australian Pelican
Title Page: Eurasian Coot

WATERBIRDS *of Australia*

Don Hadden

CONTENTS

WETLAND BIRDS

INTRODUCTION

Australia's extensive coastline and surrounding oceans play host to a wide variety of sea and shorebirds. In this book we concentrate on those species found on or near beaches, and frequenting the inland waterways. Albatrosses, procellariiformes and penguins are omitted in favour of birds more readily seen. A comprehensive selection of migratory shorebirds is illustrated.

Australia is not renowned for extensive rivers and wetland areas but nevertheless supports a fascinating variety of waterbirds, from the Jabiru (more properly the Black-necked Stork) to the elusive crakes and rails.

About 30 migratory shorebirds arrive at our beaches and mudflats each year with another 15 to 20 vagrants turning up occasionally. The larger species, such as curlews, whimbrels and godwits, have distinctive features. But, when massed at a distance, the smaller species can be difficult to identify. Another difficulty is that some will have traces of breeding plumage when they arrive; others will be in winter plumage. Before they leave in autumn, many acquire a distinctive breeding plumage. The bird you identifed in November looks very different in April.

On the whole, land birds and ourselves sleep by night and work by day. Shorebirds, and particularly migratory waders, do not follow this diurnal behavioural pattern. Their 'day' is governed by the tide. They feed when the tide is low, and when it is high they rest. As the tides change approximately an hour each cycle, so do the birds' feeding and resting rhythms. One week they will be feeding busily mid-morning then the next week that will be their sleeping time. Prior to their departure, feeding activity intensifies. Fat is deposited and body weight can increase up to 50 per cent. When they leave, many species fly for several days and nights non-stop, using their fat reserves to power them to their Asian feeding grounds. Sadly, a number of these critical areas are being reclaimed.

Not only are their migratory journeys exceptional feats of stamina and navigation but their breeding activities are extraordinary too. To make best use of the short northern summer when daylight is virtually 24 hours long, activity is frenetic. The Sanderling may mate with one male and lay a clutch of eggs, which he incubates alone. Meanwhile she mates again with another male, who again takes care of incubation and raising the chicks, although sometimes she takes responsibility herself. In this way two sets of chicks are raised while conditions are still suitable. Other species such as the Ruff have extraordinary mating systems. An area of several square metres, known as a lek, is frequented by several males who dance and leap in their selected corners, displaying their colourful ruffs and endeavouring to attract passing females. It has been said 'that these extravagantly displaying males ... bring to mind a medieval court full of strutting dandies.' These females, who are about 25 per cent smaller, take full responsibility for incubation and chick rearing.

Ibises and spoonbills are found worldwide, with about 33 species recognised. In Australia we have three ibises and two spoonbills. The scientific name of the Australian White Ibis is Threskiornis, a combination of Greek words meaning 'sacred birds'. Ibises tend to probe for food, sometimes to the full length of their bills where mud is soft. Spoonbills sweep their broad bills from side to side through water, the sensitive tip indicating prey such as aquatic insects, small fish and shrimps

Related to the ibises and spoonbills are the Ardeidae, a family including the herons, egrets, bitterns and night-herons. Twenty-three species are on the Australian list but only 14 live and breed here. The rest are vagrants, such as some night-herons and bitterns seen only on remote Christmas Island. With their long legs and long necks, these tall wading birds are easily recognised, although positively identifying the white species takes care. Cattle Egrets are almost always seen with cattle. The Eastern Great Egret and Intermediate Egret can be difficult except when seen together. It is useful to compare neck to body length. For the Eastern Great Egret neck length is one and a half times body length, while the Intermediate Egret's neck length is equal to its body length. The Little Egret always has a slender black bill. When breeding, the Eastern Great Egret also has a black bill but its large size is unmistakable and for most of the year its bill is yellow. With binoculars it may be possible to see that the gape of the Eastern Great Egret extends beyond the eye whereas the gape of the Intermediate Egret goes no farther than level with the back of the eye.

Some herons produce spectacular ornamental plumes as the breeding season approaches. A strange feature in egrets, herons and bitterns is the 'powder down feathers.' This down is used in preening. It breaks down to form a powder and is applied to feathers to remove grease. These powder down areas are usually on the breast and rump.

All heron, egret, bittern and night-heron species will stand motionless at the water's edge waiting for prey to approach. Prey is also stalked with slow movements. Some species such as Eastern Reef Egret and Little Egret dash about after prey. Sometimes herons crouch and spread their wings over the water while searching for fish. This darkens the surface of the water and presumably improves visibility or perhaps small fish move into the shade. Another technique used when wading involves the stirring up of the sea bottom with one foot, disturbing prey. The Striated Heron has been known in other parts of its range to use bait. Holding an insect just above the water, it seeks to attract fish. All species swallow prey whole; those parts unable to be digested are regurgitated as pellets. Prey is largely aquatic, but small mammals, insects and reptiles will be eaten and a small bird foraging on seeds along the edge of a stream will be quickly snapped up.

While egrets and herons are easily observed, the Rallidae—crakes and rails—are secretive and cryptically plumaged inhabitants of densely vegetated wetlands. Like bitterns, they are difficult to observe as they skulk through reeds and grasses seeking prey. Although most can fly, they are largely terrestrial and so have strong legs and feet. Often their bodies are thin, enabling them to slip through dense vegetation easily. Worldwide, there are about 140 species with 20 on the Australian list. Several of these are vagrants, with just 14 being breeding residents. There are two native-hens. Interestingly the Tasmanian Native-hen is flightless whereas the Black-tailed Native-hen is famous for its irruptions to previously uninhabited areas after inland rains have provided suitable breeding habitat. Most rails are secretive, so little is known of their social and breeding behaviour. The widespread and conspicuous Purple Swamphen, on the other hand, has been carefully studied. Breeding behaviours are remarkably varied. While monogamous pairs successfully raise chicks, at times there may be breeding groups comprising several males, a few females and assorted helpers, which may be young from the previous year, in which all males mate with all females and a nest may contain eggs from more than one female.

There is much more that could be said about our fascinating waterbirds. Two national organisations have websites that can provide more information. These are Birds Australia at www.birdsaustralia.com.au and Bird Observation and Conservation at www.boca.org.au.

Don Hadden

Australasian Gannets are renowned for their spectacular plunges into the sea as they seek small fish such as pilchards, mackerel and anchovies. They are distributed around southern coastal regions and also throughout New Zealand, from where some juveniles migrate across the Tasman Sea to Australia.

Exclusively aquatic birds, Australasian Grebes are almost never seen on land. Their legs and lobed toes are designed for swimming and are set well back, making walking difficult. After inland rains they may turn up at small ponds where they nest, but they then return to more permanent water.

An Australian Pelican flies along a foreshore. While somewhat ungainly on land, they fly remarkably well, sometimes soaring to great heights. At times they feed cooperatively—a small flock swimming together will all plunge their heads under water simultaneously.

Almost every large reed bed in Australia will have resident Australian Reed-warblers, even if there is no other suitable habitat for hundreds of kilometres. They are shy birds, but during the breeding season reed beds become alive with the cheerful song of males establishing their territories and seeking mates.

Australian Spotted Crakes, being shy birds, normally forage in and around dense aquatic vegetation. This bird has ventured a short distance from cover. The pond was quite muddy and, with each step, the bird dragged some viscous mud along on its feet.

Usually an inhabitant of creeks and rivers, Azure Kingfishers make a brilliant splash of colour as their orange breasts and azure upperparts catch the eye when they dart across the water's surface.

Smallest of the Australian rails, Baillon's Crake is found from Africa, Europe and Asia through to Australia and New Zealand. Normally they remain well hidden among swamp vegetation and only rarely venture into the open.

A Bar-tailed Godwit in non-breeding plumage. Prior to departing for their nesting grounds in Siberia, these godwits acquire bright chestnut head, neck and underparts.

Previously known as Thick-knees, stone-curlews are found virtually worldwide, especially in tropical areas. Within Australia, Beach Stone-curlews are confined to northern coastlines, especially those less frequented by humans.

Black Swans are endemic to Australia but have been successfully introduced into New Zealand. They are vegetarians feeding on aquatic plants, a stem of which can be seen by this bird's bill.

Black-faced Cormorants perch on isolated rock stacks, abandoned jetties or navigation beacons, but rarely on beaches. They are common only around Tasmania and southern coasts.

Black-fronted Dotterels forage along the edges of inland waterways throughout Australia. They eat a variety of aquatic creatures. They do not form flocks but at a muddy wetland many birds may be seen feeding on their own.

Largely a bird of northern Australia, Black-necked Storks are often found alone seeking aquatic prey in coastal and inland wetland areas. This dark-eyed bird is a male. Females have yellow eyes.

These three Black-tailed Godwits were alternately preening and resting as they waited for the high tide to ebb and uncover their feeding areas along the Karumba foreshore. This is a migratory species that breeds in Siberia.

Unlike its Tasmanian counterpart, the Black-tailed Native-hen is a strong flier. Dozens, or even hundreds, may suddenly appear on newly formed ephemeral wetlands where they breed and then move on.

A worldwide species, the Black-winged Stilt prefers shallow freshwater wetlands where it feeds on aquatic invertebrates. Usually nests are placed near water, often on boggy ground, and bravely defended by the adults should an intruder approach.

A common resident of northern coastlines, the Brahminy Kite patrols beaches seeking carrion, but will occasionally take live fish. They have been observed stealing food from other birds.

Bridled Terns are usually found across northern Australia. Western Australian residents, though, will find them along the south-west coast, where they breed on several islands.

Photographed in April, this Broad-billed Sandpiper has largely acquired breeding plumage. Within days, it will be heading north to the arctic regions of Asia.

The Brolga is sometimes known as the Australian Crane or Native Companion. Its large size and spectacular dances make it one of Australia's best known birds. It also lives and breeds in southern New Guinea.

A common coastal species, the Brown Booby is found in tropical seas right around the world. They nest on many reefs and cays across northern Australia.

Buff-banded Rails are found in a variety of wetland areas through south-east Asia to islands of the south-west Pacific. Like other members of the rail family, they are secretive but will forage in the open if they believe the coast is clear.

Chestnut Rails are little known, difficult to observe and restricted to extensive mangrove forests in the Kimberley and Northern Territory. Being inhabitants of prime estuarine crocodile habitat, few if any ornithologists have chosen to study this species in any detail.

Often known as the Lotus bird or Lily-trotter, the Comb-crested Jacana is superbly designed for walking on floating vegetation, its extremely long toes effectively distributing its weight.

A Common Greenshank at Lee Point near Darwin. They breed across Europe and Asia, migrating to many southern hemisphere countries. Rather wary birds, they are quick to fly off, with a ringing three-note 'tchu tchu tchu' call.

Sometimes known as the Brown Noddy, the Common Noddy is a tropical tern found worldwide. In Australia it is common off the Queensland coast, where it breeds on many islands.

In Australia the Common Redshank is far from common, with small numbers reaching the far northern shores of the Kimberley and Northern Territory. They are only rarely reported elsewhere. Their breeding stronghold is temperate Europe and Asia.

Common Sandpipers migrate to Australia from their breeding grounds in Europe and Asia. They have a distinctive flicking flight with wings held low. On alighting, they teeter and bob their rear end in an exaggerated manner.

A common species throughout much of the Indian and Pacific oceans, the Crested Tern can be found right around the Australian coastline. It is our second largest tern.

Breeding in the high Arctic of northern Siberia, the Curlew Sandpiper arrives in Australia in September and returns north during March. Prior to its departure, it moults into breeding plumage—its head, neck and underparts become a bright chestnut red.

Sometimes known as the Snakebird, this male Darter shows its sharp pointed bill, which it uses to pierce fish underwater. After surfacing it flicks the fish off and catches it before swallowing it head first.

The Eastern Curlew is the largest migratory wader visiting Australia. They feed by probing their massive bills into marine mudflats, where they find molluscs and crabs. Wary birds, they are the first to fly off when people approach.

An Eastern Great Egret landing on the Cairns foreshore. There are five white 'herons' in Australia. The Eastern Great Egret is the largest, with a neck one and a half times the length of its body.

Eastern Reef Egrets are exclusively marine and occur in both grey and white plumages. They are rarely seen on long unbroken beaches, preferring rocky shorelines where they seek fish in rockpools.

As its name implies, the Eurasian Coot is found from Britain through to Australia. This bird is feeding its newly hatched chicks on aquatic vegetation.

When observed in full sun, the Glossy Ibis is seen to be all brown. In poor light, they often look blackish. Their long curved bill is used for probing for aquatic invertebrates.

An almost worldwide species, this Great Cormorant is drying its wings after fishing. Underwater, they use both feet and wings to propel themselves rapidly after their prey.

Great Crested Grebes are not seen on land, their legs and feet designed for swimming not walking. Their nests are on water, usually supported by a submerged branch.

Great Knots arrive in their tens of thousands from breeding grounds in north-eastern Siberia. It seems that most of the world's population winters in Australia. In non-breeding plumage, it is a nondescript species with no distinctive features.

The Greater Sand Plover breeds across central Asia from Turkey to southern Siberia, with many thousands migrating to Australia after nesting.

Green Pygmy-geese are found on lakes and billabongs in north-eastern Australia and lowland New Guinea. Despite being known as geese, they are actually small ducks with goose-like bills.

This Grey Teal was walking from one shallow pool to another. Grey Teal may be found where there are suitable wetlands and are renowned for turning up on ephemeral waters after rain anywhere in Australia.

Grey-tailed Tattlers breed in Siberia and then migrate to Australian shores, more commonly in the north. They forage on tidal mudflats, taking crustaceans, crabs and small fish.

A worldwide species, the Gull-billed Tern may be found anywhere in Australia where there are suitable wetlands. They breed in most months of the year, always near inland lakes and waterways.

A female Hardhead is about to land on a small pool. The webbed feet touch first, allowing the bird to 'ski' to a halt. Hardheads, previously known as White-eyed Ducks, are expert divers.

Hooded Plovers endemic to Australia are found along southern coasts. They usually inhabit broad ocean beaches but are vulnerable where they have to share these with people.

Previously known as Plumed Egret, this species now has the uninspiring name of Intermediate Egret. However, this name does reflect its place between the larger Eastern Great Egret and smaller Little Egret.

Widespread in New Zealand, the Kelp Gull was starting to be observed with some regularity in Australia in the 1950s and 1960s. Today it has a patchy distribution along our southern coasts and around Tasmania.

Lesser Crested Terns frequent northern coastlines. They are distinguished from Crested Terns by their smaller size and orange bills.

A Lesser Sand Plover stands among other migratory waders that are resting during high tide. Several thousand visit Australia each year from their Asian breeding grounds.

A Little Egret lunges towards its prey. Its small size and thin black legs and bill distinguish it from other white egrets. It is a widespread species, being found from Africa through Asia to Australia.

Little Grassbirds are shy, retiring inhabitants of swamp vegetation, only briefly appearing in the open before disappearing into cover. Usually the presence of Little Grassbirds is established by hearing its plaintive high-pitched, mournful calls, all on the same pitch.

Little Pied Cormorants have stubby yellow bills and are the smallest of Australia's cormorants. The plumage of this bird has become stained from foraging in Marlgu Billabong at the Parry Lagoons area of Western Australia.

Stints are the smallest of the migratory waders to visit Australia. This Long-toed Stint is an uncommon visitor from Siberia. Its yellowish legs distinguish it from other stints.

Marsh Sandpipers breed across northern Eurasia and migrate in moderate numbers to northern Australia, with just a few reaching southern wetlands. While they may be found on tidal mudflats, they prefer freshwater wetlands.

Nankeen Night Herons are usually nocturnal, but many will forage by day. The nape plumes of this bird were flying free in the strong breeze it was facing.

Ospreys are almost exclusively marine, although a few will follow major rivers inland. They are expert at capturing surface swimming fish. Very rarely, they will eat terrestrial vertebrates.

Pacific Black Ducks become tame in city gardens but are shy and wary elsewhere. This wild bird was in a pool at Canteen Creek, a remote settlement in the Northern Territory.

Like other gull species, Pacific Gulls are scavengers seeking out stranded fish. This is the dark-eyed western form photographed at Two People's Bay in Western Australia.

Pied Cormorants are found coastally right around Australia but many birds have been reported well inland in larger lakes and rivers. Primarily fish eaters, they have also been recorded taking crustaceans such as shrimps.

Pied Herons are found in Indonesia, New Guinea and in wetlands across northern Australia. This young bird is yet to acquire its dark head cap and crest.

Pink-eared Ducks have sensitive flaps on the upper mandible, which hang below the lower mandible and presumably enhance their food-gathering potential. They inhabit inland wetlands, from small farm ponds to large lakes.

A small flock of Plumed Whistling-Ducks on a pond in the Kimberley. The distinctive upswept flank plumes distinguish this species from the Wandering Whistling-Duck.

A Purple Swamphen lunges forward as it spots a morsel of food. Purple Swamphens are omnivorous and will eat almost anything, from aquatic vegetation to frogs, small birds, insects and fruit.

A Red Knot, second left, flanked by Curlew Sandpipers waits for a high tide to recede so it can continue feeding. This bird is in breeding plumage and will soon depart for its Siberian nesting grounds.

A female Red-capped Plover on a beach near Darwin. They are also found near inland wetlands. If a predator approaches a nest, Red-capped Plovers will perform an injury-feigning display designed to lure the predator away.

Red-kneed Dotterels are widespread around suitable wetlands throughout Australia, with a few birds in southern New Guinea. They probe for various aquatic creatures and will wade or even swim if necessary.

The first rays of the morning sun touch a Red-necked Avocet busily feeding. They sweep their upturned slightly opened bills from side to side, relying on touch to locate prey.

A Red-necked Stint in non-breeding plumage stands on a rock at high tide. Once the tide has ebbed, the bird will feed busily to build up its fat reserves in readiness for its long migration to northern Siberia.

A Royal Spoonbill in flight. The dark wingtips indicate this bird has yet to acquire full adult plumage. When feeding, Royal Spoonbills sweep their partially open bills through water in broad arcs.

This Ruddy Turnstone has largely acquired its breeding plumage ready for its long flight to its nesting grounds in northern Asia. Ruddy Turnstones are circumpolar breeders and migrate to all southern hemisphere countries.

A Sacred Kingfisher in mangroves along the Kimberley coast. They may be found seeking crabs on tidal mudflats or along inland waterways, where they might feed on anything from small fish to lizards and small mammals.

A Sharp-tailed Sandpiper probes for food in a muddy wetland area near Mount Isa. Many thousands migrate to Australia from north-eastern Siberia. They can be found in both marine and inland wetlands.

A Silver Gull bathing in a shallow pool on the Cairns foreshore. Silver Gulls are probably Australia's best known shorebird, abundant on southern coasts and still quite common on tropical beaches.

Sooty Oystercatchers are found right around the Australian coastline. Generally they prefer rocky areas and avoid extensive sandy beaches. This bird has been leg-flagged and banded by ornithologists from the Broome Bird Observatory.

Unless one is familiar with the calls given by Spotless Crakes, these shy swamp rails could easily remain undetected in dense swamp vegetation. They rarely venture into the open.

Striated Herons are a worldwide marine species with numerous subspecies described. In Australia they are most common on mangrove-lined northern coastlines.

The flightless Tasmanian Native-hen is found near permanent wetlands in much of the state except the south-west. Generally found in small groups, they graze on adjacent grasslands and even on newly sprouted crops, much to the ire of farmers.

Terek Sandpipers are easily distinguished from other small sandpipers by their unusual upturned bills. Strictly coastal, especially on intertidal mudflats, Terek Sandpipers arrive in September and depart late March or early April.

Wandering Whistling-Ducks frequent deep freshwater lagoons and lakes in northern Australia. They are also found in Indonesia, New Guinea and the Philippines.

Towering above a flock of migratory waders, a Whimbrel waits for the tide to ebb so it can resume feeding. Second only in size to the Curlew, Whimbrels are rather shy and are quick to fly off with a loud, distinctive, high-pitched rapid 6/8 note call.

Massive and unmistakable in full adult plumage, the White-bellied Sea-eagle is found around the entire Australian coastline. They also occur from India, through south-east Asia to New Guinea.

A White-browed Crake wades through shallow swamp waters in search of small aquatic creatures and seeds. They are found only in suitable swamps in far north Australia.

A White-faced Heron about to take off. Sometimes erroneously called a Blue Crane, White-faced Herons are widespread throughout Australia, from marine habitats to ephemeral inland waters.

White-fronted Terns are a New Zealand species that regularly visits Australia. In the 1980s a few stayed to breed in Bass Strait. The term 'white-fronted' refers to its white forehead.

Sometimes called Pacific Heron, the
White-necked Heron is often seen foraging
alone. They occur right throughout Australia,
from small ephemeral pools and heavily
wooded waterways to intertidal mudflats.

Wood Sandpipers migrate from Eurasia to inland freshwater wetlands. They are uncommon in Australia, with most of the world's population wintering in Africa and south Asia.

Yellow-billed Spoonbills are endemic to Australia. They feed in shallow inland wetlands in preference to marine mudflats, eating aquatic insects such as backswimmers.